EVERYDAY CIRCUS

By
KATHRYN VELIKANJE
Illustrated by
Shelly Miller

LEVITY PRESS

This book uses OpenDyslexic. This font was created to help dyslexic readers. The heavy bottoms and unique character shapes help prevent letters and numbers from being confused.
Available at http://dyslexicfonts.com

Published by Levity Press
http://www.levitypress.com
Email: info@levitypress.com

ISBN-13: 978-0615681511
ISBN-10: 0615681514

To Kent, Melissa and Annie.

We don't need a family room.
Our bathroom holds us all.
The four of us, plus dog and cat,
are standing in the stall.

Kent is sitting on the toilet
while I'm making up my face.
Annie's playing with her Legos.
How I wish we had more space.

Kent's coffee cup has mold in it.
The dog has cracked a bowl.
Annie's eating mint toothpaste.
The hose has sprung a hole.

The cat is in the cupboard.
The dog's scratching his behind.
Annie's eating shaving cream.
Melissa speaks her mind.

The cat is on the counter.
The dog is in the trash.
Annie's eating my new lipstick.
And I am out of cash.

The cat is on the keyboard.
The weeds are getting high.
The dog has fleas, my home's a mess,
I think I'm going to cry.

The dog's stealing our steak dinner.
Melissa's standing on her head.
The rabbit's loose, the neighbor's mad,
at least that's what he said.

Fire-bellied toads eat crickets,
the African toad eats mice,
twenty-one pets are too much,
and both my kids have lice.

The dog chewed Annie's Barbies,
bit off their feet and arms.
Headless Barbies are not pretty.
It takes away their charms.

The cat chases our pet rabbit.
The rabbit chases our pet cat.
My call's on hold, the snake is cold,
Melissa wants a rat.

Annie's on her seventh cookie,
and she's running down the street.
My work's not done, the dog won't come,
I'm feeling really beat.

I'm dining in the bathtub,
watermelon makes me slurp.
Kent and Annie join me.
Melissa gives a burp.

My car leaks oil on the ground,
And I'm behind in school.
The dog ripped our screen door again,
chewed up the plastic pool.

We share our bed with cat and dog
and neighbor children, too.
Annie leaves crumbs in our bed
and wears my high-heeled shoes.

I had to throw my heels away,
the dog had chewed them up.
Annie dumped out all her toys
while looking for her cup.

There is litter in my hallway;
books and toys are in my bed.
Annie plays with my make-up
and smears it on her head.

Annie eats ice cream for lunch,
scatters popcorn on the floor.
The dog farts in his sleep so bad,
Kent had to shut the door.

Yellow is the toilet water
the dog laps thirstily.
It might be lemonade to him,
but still it's gross to see!

Melissa wants to be a mouse,
but God made her a girl,
who eats cheese slices by the pound,
her favorite is Cheese Swirl.

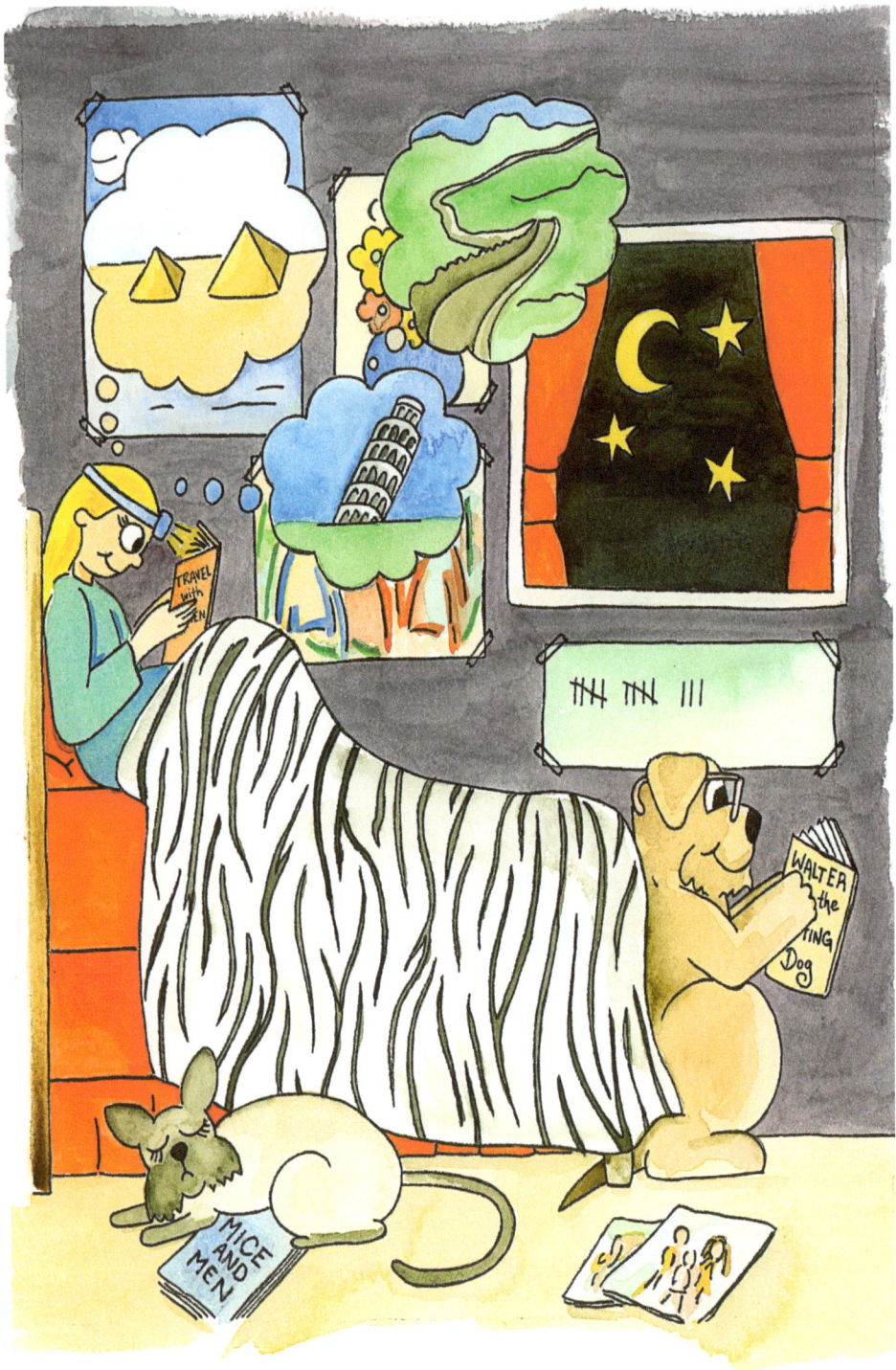

She likes to stay up late at night,
to read books endlessly.
She counts the days til school is out,
can travel happily.

Chaotic is my household.
I love my motley crew.
We don't need a family room.
Any room will do.

If you liked

EVERYDAY CIRCUS

Look for more books
by Kathryn Velikanje

COMING SOON....
Silly Willy's Alphabet

A is for Alligator

B is for Boys & Bees

C is for Crazy Cats

ABOUT THE AUTHOR

Kathryn is an American who has been teaching English in China since 2009. She graduated from the University of California at Santa Barbara with a Bachelor of Arts in Literature and has taught over 4500 ESL classes, from preschool through university as well as to teachers and doctors.

ABOUT THE ILLUSTRATOR

Shelly is a Canadian who lives in California with her husband, Nicholas, and their children. She graduated from Bowdoin College in Maine with a Bachelors in Visual Arts and was also a collegiate athlete: a two time All-American Ice Hockey center and captain of the Soccer team. She received a Masters in Education from Pepperdine University in California. She has taught math, physical education, and visual arts but is concentrating on her own art while raising her children.

www.ingramcontent.com/pod-product-compliance
Lightning Source LLC
Chambersburg PA
CBHW041241040426
42445CB00004B/111